When Morning Comes

The Dawning of a New Day!

Poetry and Prose

By Bernetha Moultrie

authorHOUSE®

AuthorHouse™
1663 Liberty Drive
Bloomington, IN 47403
www.authorhouse.com
Phone: 1 (800) 839-8640

Published by AuthorHouse 08/29/2019

ISBN: 978-1-5462-2698-7 (sc)
ISBN: 978-1-5462-2699-4 (hc)
ISBN: 978-1-5462-2700-7 (e)

Library of Congress Control Number: 2018902517

Print information available on the last page.

Any people depicted in stock imagery provided by Getty Images are models, and such images are being used for illustrative purposes only. Certain stock imagery © Getty Images.

This book is printed on acid-free paper.

Photo Credits:
Tricia Ruiz, Family Archives Collection

Scriptures are taken from the King James Version of the Bible-Public Domain.

Contents

In De Olden Days …

Life … And Living

Getting Real With God …

Love … God's Greatest Gift!

The Heavenly Marriage of The Lamb

My sister, my brother,
Shine!
With the radiant Glory of God!
From the inside out.

Heaven's "Glory Cloud"
is moving with you,
wherever you go!

Dedicated to

My Lord and Saviour Jesus Christ, who hath enabled me; for that He has counted me faithful, putting me into the ministry.

1 Timothy 1:12

My Special Prayer

For you who enjoy wholesome reading, may you be refreshed.

For you who are broken, may you be healed.

For you who are grieving, may you be comforted.

For you who are weary, may you find peace and rest.

For you who need a friend, whose name is Jesus.

For you who are lost, and in need of a Saviour.

For you who are sick, may you be made whole.

For you who walk in victory! May you be encouraged.

For you who need a moment for honest reflection, may you be renewed.

WHEN MORNING COMES
is prayerfully yours!

Introduction

Life is a journey full of adventures, with its peaks and valleys, twists and turns, "bumps" and curves.

Life: the amazement, and excitement of conception; the joy and wonder of birth; the laughter, giggles and "cooing" upon the discovery of toes-to-mouth during infancy; the sweet, wide-eyed innocence of childhood; and those awkward years of puberty!

Sandwiched within generational growth are those exciting, sometimes challenging experiences: waking up on Christmas morning! Learning to count to fifty! Reciting the Lord's Prayer without missing a word! Playing hopscotch, and running around the mulberry bush; eating peanut butter and "gooey" mayonnaise sandwiches; playing jackstones and marbles and makeshift baseball; then those teenage molding years of discovery! Pretty flirty girls and grotesquely cute boys... Life: quite interesting!

Life's journey continues with the maturing young adult's aspirations and quests for achievement: buying your first car; obtaining that revered college degree; landing that "perfect" career with the promise of promotion... and travel! Socializing with friends, and the joy of discovering "true love".... then marriage; buying your first home; motherhood... fatherhood... family togetherness... church... vacations... and grand parenting! Quite a dream, quite an adventure, quite a journey, this thing called "life".

Also along life's journey is the reality of living, with its staunch contrasts in navigating through the "highs" and "lows"... living and dying; happiness and sadness; peace and confusion; laughter and tears; pain and healing; frustrations, anger, disappointing "let downs"... these varied emotional experiences all intermingled with living, growing, maturing, and aging.

WHEN MORNING COMES will walk you through some of these experiences, some wonderfully sweet, others realistically painful… but all pointing to the glorious promise of Daybreak! Hope! The Dawning Of A New Day!

-the author

Then Comes ... Morning!

Good Morning! *Good Morning!!* **Good Morning!!!**

Good Morning!!!

"He sendeth forth his commandment upon earth: His word runneth very swiftly."
Psalm 147:15

It's A Beautiful Day!

"My voice shalt thou hear in the morning, O Lord; in the morning will I direct my prayer unto thee, and will look up."

Psalm 5:3

It's a lovely morning, a beautiful day!
I reach over, spring open the curtains.
Got to see this brand new morning!
The sun's slowly rising, peeping over the horizon.
Even the sky's waking up, all ablaze with light!

It's a lovely morning, a beautiful day!
Hey! I hear music. I hear chirping and singing!
A sound of happiness, a sound of thanksgiving!
Why, the melody's coming from a little bird, a little blue jay!

Oh, the little blue jay's just a-chirping and a-singing
And a-singing and a-chirping
At the very top of his little voice!
I listen as the other little birdies, too,
Join this little blue jay in singing, right on cue!

The little birdies are hitting the "high" notes
Then swinging to the "low" notes,
Twirling musical sounds all in between…

Amazing!
All the little birdies praising God, their Creator!
A full chorus of joyful sounds they send up to heaven;
And for every note, and for every little "chirp"
Why, these little birdies really, truly mean it!

Oh, my heavenly Father, I love you too. I do!
I worship you. I honor you. I adore you!
For you, O Lord, are holy. You are worthy
Of all the glory, of all the praise,
For your very name is holy!

A New Day!

"His compassions fail not. They are new every morning: great is thy faithfulness."

Lamentations 2:22-23

A brand new morning!
Oh, glorious new day!
God has proven his faithfulness
As new mercies he's allowing me to see.
Got the use and activity of my limbs,
All my faculties working. Hey! I'm fit and trim!

With a full stretch and a wide yawn,
I roll out of bed, fall on my knees.
Now fully awake, I whisper, "Thank you, Jesus!"
God breathes on me his comfort, his ease.
I flex my arms, move my legs,
Then stand up, start to walk,
Even hear my own voice as I begin to talk!

Thank you, Lord!
You looked after me all through the night
As your holy angels surrounded me
From my left to my right.
Lord, you protected me as I peacefully slept.
Then you touched me with your finger of love,
And through your touch today I'll be kept.

A brand new morning!
Oh, glorious day!
Lord, I feel your peace, a wonderful sweet peace,
As my eyes behold this new day of beauty,
Realizing all nature's responding in unity!
The moon has set. The sun now rises,
Ushering in abundant daylight for our daily enterprises.

A brand new morning!
Oh, glorious day!
This, our heavenly Father has given us:
A fresh start, a new beginning;
A whole brand new day!

Lord, You Filled Me Up

"But ye, beloved, building up yourselves on your most holy faith, praying in the Holy Ghost."

Jude 20

O my heavenly Father,
You filled me up with your Holy Spirit again,
Imparting to me a new level of courage
Needed for witnessing to every man.

O Lord, you filled me up of yourself
With your power,
Your glory,
Your greatness!

You breathed on me your comforting breath,
Opening up more of your will,
More of your sweetness.

O heavenly Father! You filled me with your Holy Spirit
Until my very cup has overflowed
With your joy, your beauty, your peace
To spill over to others,
Sharing your Spirit increase.

Lord, you poured into me your Holy Spirit
To tell everybody Jesus is our salvation!
That on Calvary, you shed your precious blood
For all the little children,
For their daddies, and for their mommas.

Thank you, Lord, for your precious Holy Spirit!
For your grace, for your mercy, for your beauty.
Thank you for filling me over and over again,
Giving me your strength and your power
For every challenge to win!

Somebody's Praying

"And pray for one another, that ye may be healed. The effectual, fervent prayer of the righteous availeth much."

James 5:16b

Somebody's praying!
I can feel it;
Asking God to bless, to intervene
For their son, for their daughter,
To lead them, guide them in fulfilling their dreams.

Somebody's praying!
And their prayers are penetrating the atmosphere,
Breaking up confusion, breaking up clouds of despair
With the powerful, concentrated Word of God
That hits the target, casting down error from the air.

Somebody's praying!
Releasing God's blessings
According to His holy Word:
Blessings in the home, that needs will be met,
That smiles and laughter and joy will be felt.

Somebody's praying!
Proclaiming God's Word of salvation
For every family, every neighbor,
For countries throughout the world;
Bringing peace and harmony and unity
From our heavenly Father, our Creator.

Blessed be the Lord, who daily loadeth us with benefits.
Even the God of our salvation, Se'lah.
—Psalm 68:19

God Speaks to My Heart

Date:

Scripture Text:

Scripture Text:

My Thoughts or Prayer Request:

Momma's Biscuits

"She riseth also while it is yet night, and giveth meat to her household."
Proverbs 31:15

It's morning!
We wake up to the sweet aroma of bacon frying
And our momma's humming as she cooks.
Then the alarm (Momma's voice) goes off!
"Time to get up!" Momma calls.
"Get up! Time to get ready for school!"

And this morning, same as every morning
Momma's in the kitchen,
Cooking us a good ole' hot breakfast,
Grits, bacon, and eggs and pipin' hot biscuits!

Tomorrow morning? Same thing with a twist:
Grits, sausage and eggs, and her pipin' hot biscuits!
The next day? You guessed it!
Grits, liver and onions, and Momma's hot biscuits!
And that liver gravy, real tasty over my grits,
Just right to sop up with my hot biscuit!

And then there's suppertime on Friday!
What else? Grits, hot fish, and pipin' hot biscuits!
Eating to our heart's content,
Hot biscuits and fried fish, 'til it all just went!

Momma's biscuits?
Good any day, any time, with anything!
Stewed chicken 'n' dumplings,
Fresh butter beans 'n' dumplings,
Peas w'green snaps 'n' dumplings,
Hot biscuits 'n' fried chicken,
Hot biscuits 'n' pork chops,
Hot biscuits 'n' liver puddin',
Hot biscuits dripping with butter to sop in syrup,
Or just plain hot biscuits filled with fig preserves!

Nothing like our momma's hot biscuits
To get the day started
Or to have on the dinner table.
Satisfied Momma's biscuits make our stomachs,
And contented her biscuits make our hearts!

Favorite Recipes

Momma's Homemade Biscuits

2 cups self-rising flour
2 teaspoons sugar
1/3 cup shortening
milk to bind

Put flour and sugar in medium bowl.
Cut in shortening with fork or pastry blender until well blended.
Add milk, stirring in slowly.
Knead lightly.
Form biscuits in palm of hand or roll out and cut with biscuit cutter.
Bake at 400 degrees until golden brown.
Brush with butter if desired.

Momma's Sweet Potato Pie

6 large sweet potatoes
2 1/3 cups sugar
1 1/2 sticks butter
1/3 cup evaporated milk
1 1/2 teaspoons nutmeg
1 teaspoon cinnamon
1 tablespoon vanilla
5 tablespoons self-rising flour

Boil sweet potatoes, drain well, and peel.
Mash, and then beat with an electric beater to remove strings
Stir in sugar, butter, milk, nutmeg, cinnamon, and vanilla.
Add self-rising flour. Mix well.
Divide between two or three unbaked pie shells.
Bake at 350 degrees until crust is brown and batter bubbles in center.
For variety, coconut, well drained pineapple, or chopped nuts may be
Added to the batter.

Daddy's Lunch Bucket

"Children are an heritage of the Lord ... Happy is the man that hath his quiver full of them."

Psalm 127:3a, 5a

Our daddy was a hardworking man,
The breadwinner for our family.
A good example of fatherhood, he did stand;
A provider for his wife and children, a family man.

Our daddy would leave for work early in the morning,
Carrying his lunch bucket, packed by our momma;
Filled with leftovers from last night's meal
Along with her surprise or two to insure he got his fill.

Sometimes while Daddy was at work, we'd get into a rumble,
Disobeyed Momma, or fussed too much, especially our brothers!
"Just wait 'til your daddy gets home!" exclaims Momma.
Oh boy! This means we're really in trouble!

But when we'd see our daddy coming,
Whether in the house, or outside playing,
Or the boys just "roaming"
When our daddy was sighted coming home,
You can hear our squeals of excitement:
"Daddy! Daddy! Daddy's home!!!"

We drop everything! And run to meet our daddy!
To receive his pat on the head or his "hey!" or perhaps his hug.
Then we dive into his lunchbox! And open his coffee mug;
There's sure to be a cracker, a half sandwich,
A stick of gum, or something!
And all of us share,
'Cause it's from our daddy's lunch bucket!

Daddy's home!!!
Running to meet him from every which way,
Seeing our daddy, and telling him "hey!"
Then scrambling for his lunch bucket.
Now this really makes our day!

Suppertime

"Thy wife shall be as a fruitful vine by the sides of thine house: thy children like olive plants round about thy table."

Psalm 128:3

It's suppertime! Time to eat.
The big girls help Momma set the table,
The plates, the forks, and the spoons for the littlest ones,
And for our Kool-Aid, ice cubes in the glasses or the tumblers.

Momma takes up our food,
Fixing Daddy's plate first.
Then she places Daddy's plate at his seat
At the head of the dinner table;
And going around, all our plates she fills
As we anxiously wait, for supper is our thrill!

With faces washed, hands nice and clean,
We're now seated around the table.
Don't dare act mean!
All hands folded, heads all bowed,
For our good meal we give God the honor.
Our daddy prays the grace of thanksgiving
For the food we receive, our Heavenly Father's provision.

Amen! Daddy ends the grace with a Scripture verse,
And Momma, too, says her verse from the Bible.
And one by one, we children all follow:
"The Lord is my shepherd, I shall not want",
To "Jesus wept!" recited by the littlest one;
THEN WE EAT!!
A simple meal, mixed with love from our Momma!

We watch our manners, no "smacking" our lips,
No chewing food with our mouth open;
No reaching across the table, but "please pass the bread"
We ask for seconds, remembering to say "please Ma'am",
For at supper time, a must were our table manners!

"Sister, "Do you want your piece of meat?" I quietly ask,
And in return, I give her a little corner of my bread,
"Ouch!" … my sister stabs me in the side!
"Ouch!" … with her sharp "elbow jab"!
Oh my! We've blown it …
That does it for us trying to behave!

One by one we finish our supper,
Then excuse ourselves, still being
"proper"
"Momma, I enjoyed that!"
Each of us would say,
As we skip off from the table,
To finish homework, or go back to play.

Now this was supper time at our house ...
A time to say Grace,
A time for Bible verses,
And good table manners,
A time of togetherness ...
With our Daddy, and our Momma!

God Speaks To My Heart

Date:

Scripture Text:

Scripture Text:

My Reflections/ Prayer Request:

And A Child
Shall
Lead Them

"The wolf also shall dwell with the lamb, and the leopard shall lie down with the kid; and the calf and the young lion and the fatling together; and a little child shall lead them." Isaiah 11:6

It's Christmas!

Joy To The World! The Lord Is Come!
Silent Night! Holy Night! The carols are sung;
Beautiful fruit baskets all filled with treats,
We give to the "shut-ins" as a special treat.

Jingle bells! Jingle bells!
Ringing in the air,
And a wish for snowflakes for that added flair;
It's Christmas!!!
You can feel it everywhere!
As joy and excitement, and laughter we share.

The Christmas cantatas and programs, such a treat,
Heralding beautiful carols of the Christ Child,
Holy and sweet;
The choirs all robed in red and white,
As pageants showcase that starry night.

Now Momma's got the fruit cakes all done,
The coconut and potato pies, too;
The turkey's browning 'til morning comes,
Sour cream pound cake, chocolate layer cake … Umm-Um!

The whole house smells of Christmas!
Apples, oranges, pecans, walnuts and candies,
As little "Baby Jesus" rests sweetly in the manger;
With pretty wrapped presents all around,
More than a little heart can handle!

"Sister, we got to go to sleep, it's almost Christmas!
You sleep, Sister?"
"Yea", she whispers … "What about you?"
"Well, my heart's going thump 'de thumb, thump 'de thump,
Too excited, 'cause it's almost Christmas morning!"

"I want some water!" chirps little baby sister,
"O.K. You can get some water, but don't you peep!
It's not daylight yet, little sister,
And right now, we're supposed to be sleep."

Pitty pat, pitty pat, her little feet we hear,
Skipping back to bed, her voice all filled with cheer:
"I saw a doll baby, and a tea set too!
And Bubba's got what looks like a new pair shoes!"

Momma and Daddy, can we get up now?
"Yes", says our Daddy, "but keep the noise down".
LIGHTS ON!!!
To the living room we race!
It's Christmas!!!
Hey … There's toys all over the place!

"Look! I gotta tea set, and a pretty bride doll!
And look! Tangerines and apples, all kinda fruit;
Two pairs of bobby socks, a pretty sweater, too,
And some crayons, and new coloring book!"
"I gotta tricycle, and there's a red wagon to pull!"
Shouts Bubba to our little baby brother;
"And you gotta dump truck, too,
"And look! Here's my new pair of shoes!"

"Let's see the presents, we got them, too!
Oh, a scarf from Aunt Lizbeth,
A box of oranges from Uncle Gene,
And socks from Me'Me'
And more candy and pecans, whoop-eee!

"O.K. let's go outside, and see what the others' got!"
The whole neighborhood's excited as cheers' spread about;
Doors swinging open, and "Merry Christmas!" we hear,
Everybody's jolly, because Christmas is here!

Bright red and blue bicycles, all shiny and new,
Little girls on roller skates, seeing what they can do;
Sweet little baby dolls that walk, and smile, and cry,
Toy cowboy guns all the little boys love to try!
Brand new sweaters and coats,
And ear muffs, too;
Model airplanes, and tiny little boats;
Oh, the children are so happy, as we hear fireworks, too!

It's Christmas!!!
What a wonderful time of the year,
To celebrate the birth of our Lord Jesus,
And to spread Christmas cheer!

Easter

The flowers are blooming,
The grass so pretty and green;
Easter is coming,
Our whole house is shiny and clean!

Spring cleaning, always Momma's "must",
All to get rid of winter's dust;
Washing windows, mopping and waxing floors, soaking the blinds,
Washing and starching Priscilla curtains, and then those to iron.

And then Momma's to her sewing!
Making our pretty frilly dresses …
Pink, and yellow, and blue, with satin bows,
Then to crinoline slips, some half, some whole.

Brand new ribbons for our hair, atop baby-doll curls,
Patent leather shoes and pretty socks,
A must for little girls!
New suits for the boys, and bow ties, too;
Black or brown leather shoes, and new socks to boot!

Dyeing Easter eggs to fill our baskets,
Easter egg candy, and jelly beans in colorful plastic;
Then off to rehearsal to practice our speeches,
The Easter egg hunt and picnic, with goodies and sweets.

And then it's Easter Sunday morning! And we're off to church,
To learn about Christ's crucifixion, and His resurrection to worship.
To see all the other children, all dressed up to,
To show off our pretty new dresses and bows, and hats and shoes.

Then the "nervous time" came!
All dressed up to sing and recite ... this is *it,* no more games!
Take a bow, do your curtsey, stand up straight, speak loud and clear,
So everybody in the church can hear, even from the rear!

Jesus is risen!
Oh children listen!
This is what Easter's all about,
And that's why we sing and shout!

To celebrate Christ's death, burial and resurrection,
To thank Him for taking our place in the crucifixion;
To say, "Thank you Jesus, for dying for me,
That I might have life, for all eternity."

God Speaks To My Heart

Date:

Scripture Text:

Scripture Text:

My Reflections/Prayer Request:

Summer Time - Play Time

"He maketh peace in thy borders, and filleth thee with the finest of the wheat."

Psalm 147:14

Good Times
Last day of school !!!
Summertime!
Three whole months to play,
Having tons and tons of fun
Playing hopscotch, and doll house;
And baseball, even jackstones!

Saturday's a special treat,
That's when Momma does something different;
She pulls out the frying pan, the meal, flour and milk,
Yes! It's Saturday .. we get pancakes for breakfast!

Now we children were very creative,
Thinking of fun ways to spend our day:
Building a whole grocery store,
Using pine straw, and cornflake boxes,
Soup cans, and soda pop bottles;
Then having "church", our brother the preacher,
And we, the "Hallelujah" followers!

We pick juicy red and yellow plums,
And luscious sweet blackberries;
And from the garden, peas, butter beans,
And bright red tomatoes;
Really good eatin' the whole summer long,
Even had dessert every day - ice cold watermelon!

Playing Baseball
We get with all our playmates on the street,
And in a big "huddle" we all meet;
Picking this one, or that one, on our team,
We play "serious" baseball, for to win, we do mean!

First base, second base, third base, all covered,
The pitcher, those in the field, everybody's included!
Then Batter Up!!!
Using a "flat" piece of board for our bat,
Hey, anybody can hit a home run,
The board's just that fat!

We run, we holler, we scream,
Win the game? It will be our team!
Game tied!!!
We've got to play some more,
Until we hit another home run,
Or either "break" that score!

Prayer Time …
Well, It's noon time, twelve o'clock!
Time now to pray.
So we "hose down", and wash our hands;
Got to pause now, from baseball,
So we can say our prayers;
Always at our house,
With our Momma standing near.

"Our Father, who art in heaven" we all pray,
"The Lord is my shepherd, I shall not want",
Our playmates, too, would say;
I mean the whole Lord's prayer,
The whole twenty-third Psalm!

And Back To Baseball!
Then off to finish the game!
But sometimes our Mommas?
Well, they get these "bright" ideas,
And actually go and change our good plans!
So everybody to his own house,
To relax, to eat, to do whatever our Momma say,
For the rest of our whole good day!

But now! It's six o'clock or so,
In the evening, the cool of the day;
Hey! We've got the lowest score!
We've got a game to finish!
Back to the "huddle"
To figure out what to do;
Baseball we do love,
The whole summer through!

Sunday Morning Family Prayer

"This is the generation of them that seek him, that seek thy face, O God of Jacob."

Psalm 24:6

Well, t's Sunday!
Early in the morning,
Time for family prayer,
With our Daddy and our Momma;
Everybody to the living room,
We kneel down at our chair,
As our Daddy begins his looong… prayer!

Now this time,
On Sunday morning?
Hey, we act right!
Our Daddy's in charge!
Besides, he prays long enough as it is,
And it will really help us,
Just to be quiet,
And very, very still.

Then Daddy prays,
"Lord, we thank you
For keeping us all week long,
From all hurt, harm, and danger;
You brought us this far,
And for this, Lord,
We're so thankful."

Then after his looong … prayer,
Our Daddy reads a scripture from the Bible,
Completing our devotions
On Sunday morning,
A very special hour.

Now those early days,
Those simple times for prayer,
We're convinced have kept us
In our loving God's care.

For no matter where,
Regardless how old,
God's Word, and the prayers in our life
Have proven to us more precious than gold!

God Speaks To My Heart

Date:

Scripture Text:

Scripture Text:

My Reflections/Prayer Request:

"Whosoever therefore shall humble himself
as this little child, the same is greatest in the
kingdom of heaven.
And whoso shall receive one such little child
in my name receiveth me."
St. Matthew 18:4-5

Children's Bedtime

"And all thy children shall be taught of the LORD; and great shall be the peace of thy children."

Isaiah 54:13

It's bedtime!
We kneel yet again,
To say our prayers;
"Now I lay me down to sleep …
"Stop hunching me!"

My sister, with that "innocent" look of hers,
Peeks up from prayer, rolling her eyes,
Like she hadn't done a thing!
She winces as I yell out again,
"You hit me!"
Uh huh, just a little bit too loud!

"Now y'all behave"! says Momma (or Daddy),
Whichever one's watching as we pray; "All
right … you move down some … this way;
Now start over; Now you can say your prayers."

We squirm, and we sigh …
Settling down,
Refolding our hands,
Bowing our heads,
Closing our eyes;
This time? We will get it right!

"Now I lay me down to sleep,
I pray the Lord, my soul to keep…"
Going straight through, this time,
And without even an "eye peep",
Saying perfectly every single line!

Cause it's serious time,
This saying our prayers,
Asking God to bless us,
Also people everywhere.

"And Lord, please bless Momma and Daddy,
And all our sisters and brothers";
We name them all,
One by one, and name by name!

"And please bless everybody
In the whole wide world! In
Jesus' name I pray, Amen."

Homeroom Morning Devotions

"For He hath strengthened the bars of thy gates; he hath blessed thy children within thee."

Psalm 147:13

8:15!
The last bell rings!
Just one more "Hey there!"
With that final bang! and Slam! of locker doors;
Whew! Now In our home room class!
We're all seated, and quiet, and in order;
Our school day now begins.

We wait for the sound of the intercom,
It's our principal's voice:
"Good morning!"
"Today's devotions will be led by Homeroom class 6-B
Please listen attentively;
Everyone should be seated."

The well-rehearsed scripture is read by our classmate,
And prayer, also offered by a student, every word in place;
Then we recite the Pledge of Allegiance to the Flag,
Led by the Student Council;
Finally, the voice of our principal we hear again,
Giving us directions for the day,
Along with very important announcements.

This is the moment when every teacher,
Every student, every child
All pause as "one",
And quietly worship God for a while;
To honor our Heavenly Father,
The Creator, who is Sovereign;
To sit together in His presence,
To receive His love, and also His pardon.

Morning devotions at school …
Another discipline in molding us children in positive ways:
Love for God and our great country,
Good manners, honor for our teachers;
Also mutual respect for fellow classmates.

Lasting benefits …
Astuteness at public speaking, strong in leadership skills.
Insuring soundness of character, and mental stability;
Showing us how to acknowledge God,
The giver of all good things: each and every ability.

The Child, Christ Jesus

"Therefore the Lord himself shall give you a sign: Behold, a virgin shall conceive, and bear a son, And call his name Immanuel. Butter and honey shall he eat, that he may know how to refuse evil, and choose good."

Isaiah 7:14-15

The child, Christ Jesus,
The Begotten One from the Father
Even he himself from his parents learned discipline;
As a child, he made the right choices:
To be obedient,
To pray,
And to honor God's Holy Day.

The child, Christ Jesus,
Learned a trade from Joseph,
His earthly "father"
He became a skilled carpenter,
Following after his role model.

The child, Christ Jesus,
Learned the scriptures,
God's Holy Word;
And at the tender age of twelve,
His intellect baffled even the "learned" scholars,
The doctors and the lawyers!

"Therefore the Lord himself shall give you a sign"
This, a prophetic word,
Pointing to the coming of our Lord and Saviour, Jesus Christ:
His name to be Immanuel, "God with us",
Fulfilling his destiny, his reason for being, his purpose in life.

Coming from heaven, down to us!
Living here on earth, among us;
Sharing in our humanity,
Feeling our infirmities;
Knowing our hurts, our pains;
Imparting to us His great salvation!

Bringing to us true hope!
Delivering us from bondage,
Setting us free from sin;
Healing us from without,
Cleansing us within.

"Hear, O Israel: the Lord our God is one Lord:
And thou shalt love the Lord thy God with all thine heart, and with
all thy soul, and with all thy might.

And these words, which I command thee this day, shall be in thine
heart.

And thou shalt teach them diligently unto thy children, and shalt talk
of them when thou sittest in thine house, and when thou walkest by the
way, and when thou liest down, and when thou riseth uo."

Deuteronomy 6:4-7

Show The Children!

"And that from a child thou has known the holy scriptures, which are able to make thee wise unto salvation through faith which is in Jesus Christ."

2 Timothy 3:15

Show the children!
How to choose the good and better things;
That the right way is not always the "feel good" way,
But the right way insures for them stability,
And a bright future, as right choices they begin to make.

Show the children!
How to reverence God,
The Creator of heaven and earth;
Show them by example:
Respect for their elders, and for their peers;
Building within them humility, and upright living,
Insuring for them peaceful hearts, and a spirit of sharing.

Show the children!
The importance of prayer,
By praying with them;
A love for the scriptures,
By reading God's word with them;
Then living for God
In front of them!

God Speaks To My Heart

DATE:

SCRIPTURE TEXT:

SCRIPTURE TEXT:

MY REFLECTIONS/ PRAYER REQUEST:

Walking With God Through the Valley

"When thou passest through the waters,
I will be with thee,
And through the rivers,
they shall not overflow thee:
When thou walkest through the fire,
Thou shalt not be burned;
Neither shall the flame kindle upon thee."
Isaiah 43:2

When It Ain't So Good

Healing From Bitterness In The Loss of a Child

"He healeth the broken in heart, and bindeth up their wounds."
Psalm 147:3

It's morning …
I'm awake.
Touching my stomach, suddenly, I remember:
"Oh! Oh! My baby! I lost my baby!
I'll just go back to sleep …"

The doctor walks in,
"I'm sorry" he says;
Hearing him, in my heart, I scream,
"Sorry!!! My baby's gone,
And you say you're sorry?!!" …
I'm going back to sleep.

"Oh Lord, Oh Lord; Oh Lord, Oh L*ord*
Why? Why did you take my baby?"
I reach for my Bible, running my hands over it …
"Lord help me, please help me to understand!"

My husband walks in,
So handsome, so well groomed, as he always is;
And he smells sooo … good!
But his eyes are watery, full of concern;
"You o.k.?" He asks softly;
He reaches for my hand … "You o.k.?
You had a terrible night, almost lost you;
You o.k.?"

"I don't know", I whispered,
"You were going to be a Daddy!"
He grins … I grin …
We both just grin, and grin, and grin!
And then we break into a laugh!
God has blessed our love! We grin again!
Then silence …
We *were* going to have our baby …

Hours later, alone again, I ask the Lord, "Why?
Why did you take my baby?"
I try to read a verse of scripture … can't concentrate …
"Lord, help me to understand!"

Holding my Bible close,
I whisper, "Lord, I wasn't bothering you by asking,
Yet you blessed us, and I conceived … Then you took my baby … Why?"

"I didn't take your baby," I hear God say;
"Your baby is with me."
Oh. OK… My baby is with the Lord.
But it hurts… oh, how it hurts!

I open my bible, It falls to Luke 9:51-56
The people did not receive (accept) the disciples, nor our Lord Jesus;
The disciples say to Jesus,
"Will you just call down fire from heaven, and destroy them?"
"That's not how I am," answered Jesus to his disciples;
"I did not come to destroy men's lives, but to save them;

Then Jesus began to speak to my heart from John 10:10
"It is the thief that comes to steal, to kill, and to destroy:
I am come that they might have life, and have it more abundantly."
I hear again, "I did not take your baby. Your baby is with me."

I flip my Bible again; amazingly the page falls to John 11:25
"I am the resurrection, and the life:
He that believeth in me, though he were dead, yet shall he live."
Then I hear my Lord say again,
"I am the giver of life … Your baby is with me …"

The Lord continued to minister to my heart:
"Get rid of the root of bitterness."
I respond, "I'm not bitter."
I hear again, "Get rid of the root of bitterness."
"I'm not bitter, I'm just trying to understand…."

A third time, I hear "Get rid of the root of bitterness,
Lest it spring up, and trouble you, and thereby many
be defiled" (Hebrews 12:15)
And this time… yes this third time, I respond,
"O.K. Lord, if you say I have bitterness, then you'll have to help me."
"Help me, Lord please help me!"

A day or so later, I wake up, sobbing,
"My baby! …My baby! …"
My husband holds me close, not much to say;
I sob even more… "My baby!"

My inside hurt Soo. … Soo … bad …
But I give it all, it all to you, Jesus!
And somehow, within this "mixture" of emotions,
I come to a little kind of understanding
About this "root of bitterness"
As our God, so faithful, and so gentle,
Began His walk with us, through this ordeal.

Yes, our God was there "ahead of time"
Before the wounds could take root, and we die.
He walked with us, pouring into us His oil of healing,
Helping us in Him. To keep on believing.

It was to be a year or so later:
I walk into a hospital room;
A young mother is weeping.
She has just lost her unborn baby.
Holding her hand, I just let her cry …

After a while, I say to her softly, "Your baby is o.k.
Your baby is with the Lord, and God's got great big arms,
And He's holding your baby."
Then I say to her, "He's taking care of you, too."

Slowly, the young mother begins to relax …
Somehow we both become wrapped within this powerful love of God!
And it was in that moment, I knew… I really knew…
I myself, was truly healed!

I now know that sharing in this young mother's loss
Would not be possible,
Unless I myself am healed
From my own hurt and loss!

Thank you my Heavenly Father,
For your love, your urging, your healing!
Thank you my Lord,
For your mercy, your patience, your provision;
Your healing is very, very real;
Able to prevent deep roots of bitterness from appearing.

Thank you Jesus!
For you are surely able to bear every burden,
You really do share in every care...
You, O Lord, bring wellness to the whole heart!

God Speaks To My Heart

Date:

Scripture Text:

Scripture Text:

My Reflections/Prayer Request:

Be Still

"Be still, and know that I am God: I will be exalted among the heathen, I will be exalted in the earth."

Psalm 46:10

Be still,
Know that I'm God,
Here's my hand, powerful to heal
Rest in me, your problems I'll resolve
For I'm your Saviour, I am God.

Be still,
Know that I'm God;
See here my nail-pierced feet, with steady direction,
Gone before you, I've already trod;
Walk with me, for I guide with my staff, and with my rod;
I'm your Saviour, I am God.

Be still,
Know that I'm God;
See here my wounded side,
That purchased your victory!
Stay close beside me,
My presence for you a comfort,
My presence for you the assurance
That I'm your Saviour, I am God.

Be still,
Know that I'm God;
I'm breathing into you new life,
My sweet Holy Spirit,
The very breath of God!
Whispering to you my Forever Love,
For I'm your Saviour, I am God.

Shhh! ... Quiet! ... Be still ...
Shhh! ... Rest! ... Be still ...
Be still ... ...

Be still ... And know ... I AM GOD!

You Took Your Flight!

God's Comforting Presence During Life's Final Exit of Spouse

"The Lord is close to the broken hearted; he rescues those whose spirits are crushed."

Psalm 34:18

"Precious in the sight of the LORD is the death of his saints."

Psalm 116:15

I hold your hand …
So still, yet so warm;
Your hands … Even now assuring me
That we are so connected in love …
A love that remains sealed by our God above.

I stroke your head …
Trying to ease your pain,
To calm any fear;
Assuring you, I am here.
Holding you… Loving you….
Loving you… My husband dear.

So many unanswered questions!
And doctors and nurses everywhere!
But Honey, I've got to hold on…
Be strong for you… for me… for us;
So questions??? Just can't go there.

"I am with you," our God has said,
"And I'll be with you, Even to the end".
So, here we are … here we are …
And our Faith in God? There's just no "bend".

"I'm here, Honey," I say softly,
I squeeze your hand, again …
"Oh, if you could just say something, anything …
So I can hear your voice, just once more, again!"

Family, friends, church family, are all here, standing close,
All here, supporting you, because you are so loved!
So quiet, we all are, trusting God, speaking and believing His word,
Knowing somehow. … we must release you to Almighty God.

"Oh my husband, my husband"…
I choke, and whisper as I see the monitor "bottom out"
My husband!!!!!
Then, you hesitated!!! Oh! In that very moment,
You answered… and lingered… In love to me…
For one last… final fleeting… moment.
Then… finally… I say,
"Love you Honey, I'll see you in the morning".

Then so sweetly, so gently,
You fell asleep, into the arms of your Heavenly Father,
So peaceful … you took your flight,
Right straight into the joyful presence of God!

My Husband…
All your life, you have believed the Lord;
All your life, you have lived for Him,
Believing and trusting His Word;
And now it's God's Very Word we see,
Sweetly swiftly escorting you,
"Absent from the body, present with the Lord."

Heaven welcomed you!
Heaven… That we loved to talk about, for which we lived;
Heaven… full of joy and laughter, that is so "you"
Heaven… you're there, and we're here,
Trusting our God to see us through.

Thank you Jesus! For sweet memories,
Thank you, Jesus! For your divine help. …
Guiding us all the way from earth to glory,
Our reason to keep on living a life that is holy!

One Fleeting Moment!

Reflections & Blessed Hope in the loss of a sibling

"And God will wipe away all tears from their eyes; and there shall be no more death, neither sorrow, nor crying; neither there shall be any more pain ..."

Revelation 21:4a

ONE MOMENT ...
One fleeting moment ... then SWOOSH ! ! !
This moment is over ... Gone ... No more ... Forever.

ONE MOMENT ...
Here in my hands ...
To giggle with you ... run and play with you ...
To chat and chuckle with you ...
And sing a song ... in our own way ... with you ...
For one moment.

ONE GOD-GIVEN MOMENT!
Now ... at this time ...
To be care free with hearty laughter ...
To applaud you ... to see your big winning smile ...
To touch your hand ...
And you touch mine ...

FOR ONE MOMENT…
To talk about every thing… any thing…
To be with you in this earth again…
For just one moment…
And then, you can go back to sleep….
It'll be O.K. ….
Restful, peaceful sleep in Jesus…
After one moment…

But Oh … I HAD THIS MOMENT!
In time! I had it!
And then … SWOOSH!!!
Over … Gone … No more this moment …
No more … forever. .. in this space called "time" …

So we'll just have to wait… Patiently wait…
'Till we can play… and laugh… and sing…

In our own then excellent melodious way
And have our good little talks and grins … and laughter …
When we get together again … In Heaven …
IN GOD's time … Throughout ALL ETERNITY!!!
Amen.

As You Go Before Me

The Survivor's Blessed Hope

"He that overcometh shall inherit all things; and I will be his God, and he shall be my son."

Revelation 21:7

As you go before me
Into the presence of our Holy God,
To sweet rest, and happiness, and peace;
In time, as you walk amidst the loveliest flower blossoms,
Every now and then, may you think of me.

As you go before me,
Taking in the beautiful, awesome view of heaven,
This Is God's wonderful surprise for you!
As the lively green grass and vibrant, colorful flowers
All bring smiles to you, beyond believing …

Your love for all the gentle animals
I know fills your heart with laughter and glee!
As you walk along the winding, shady green paths,
At times in awe, bowing your knee.

As you go before me,
To become a part of the great cloud of witnesses,
All the saints who've won life's battles,
And you now joining them,
Yourself having won the victory!

Oh the joy! Oh the glory!
As you bathe in the all-consuming love of God;
All things beautiful, all together lovely!
This is what you lived for, why you lived holy.

You fell asleep, to wake up in glory!
I can only imagine your huge smile,
Your chuckles, your sighs of relief
As you exclaim with your excitement,
"Thank you, Jesus! Thank you, Thank you Jesus!

As you go before me,
We have a hope!
Yes our Blessed Hope,
That in that day, when the trump of God shall sound,
We'll be raptured together, forever joy to be found!

God Speaks To My Heart

Date:

Scripture Text:

Scripture Text:

My Reflections / Prayer Request:

*Fear thou not, for I am with thee; be not
dismayed, for I am thy God; I will strengthen thee;
yea, I will help thee; yea, I will uphold thee with
the right hand of my righteousness."
Isaiah 41:10*

Go! ... Live!

"The living, the living, he shall praise thee; as I do this day."

Isaiah 38:19

GO!
For your loved one. ... LIVE!
Tell others of the goodness of Jesus,
How He is a healer of the heart,
A soothing comforter, a faithful provider.

GO!
Tell them about the 'Door" to Eternal Life!
That Jesus is the way, the truth, and the life;
And when in His Name, we're baptized,
Our sins are washed away,
Along with any strife.

GO!
Tell them about heaven's precious Holy Spirit!
The very breath of God, that brings comfort
In time when needed;
His Spirit that guides and gives power, yes the ability
To live holy every day, every minute, every hour.

GO! ... LIVE!
Offer your voice in praises to God!
In the morning, at noon, in the evening,
Give all glory to God!
The maker of heaven and earth;
For praising Him will bring new life,
And thanking Him in all things,
Gives new meaning!

"He shall feed his flock like a
shepherd: he shall gather the
lambs with his arm, and carry
them in his bosom, and shall
gently lead those that are with
young."   Isaiah 40:11

God Speaks To My Heart

Date:

Scripture Text:

Scripture Text:

Reflections/Prayer Request:

"Evening, and morning, and at noon will I pray, and cry aloud: and he shall hear my voice."

Psalm 55:17

In De Olden Days ...

"DE WAY DE OLE PEOPLE WUDA SAID IT"

featuring

THE GULLAH LANGUAGE
and the POST-SLAVERY DIALET

One generation shall praise thy works to
another, and shall declare thy mighty acts.
Psalm 145:4

Tank Ya' Lawd!

Praises To Almighty God

"My help cometh from the Lord, which made heaven and earth."
Psalm 121:2

Tankya' Lawd!
T'ankya', t'ankya' t'ankya'!
Ya' brung us dis fuh, t'ankya'!
Ya' made a way out 'en no way, t'ank ya'!
Ya' brung us tru dangis seen 'en unseen,
T'ankya' Lawd!

Lawd, ya' put food on de table, t'ank ya'!
Ya' put clo' dese on de back, t'ank ya'!
Ya' put shoes on de foots, t'ank ya'!
T'ankya' ri ni Lawd! T'ankya'!

Lawd, ya' gimme life, helt, 'en strent, t'ank ya'!
Fuh de use 'en activity uh mah limbs, t'ank ya'!
Fuh de 'bility tah see, walk, 'en talk…
HUP! T'ank ya' Lawd! T'ankya' Lawd'! T'ank ya'!

T'ankya' Lawd!
Fuh all mah fam'ly, t'ank ya'!
Fuh me wife, en all mah chillun, t'ankya' Lawd!
Fuh mah Ma'mmie 'en mah Poppa, t'ank ya'!
Fuh mah sistahs 'en mah brothuhs, t'ank ya'!
En all mah neeces en mah nephoos, t'ank ya'!
Fuh all mah cuzins … 'en fuh all mah ann'tees … 'en uncles,
T'ankya' Lawd!
For all mah nabors. … and mah friends 'en luv ones,
T'ankya'!

Ni Lawd … not fuh sich lawng prayah
But'n we ask ya' bless'ns on de whol' wide wurld,
Cuzsho'nuf us'un all inneeda'ya!
'En fuh all deese heah blessins'
Lawd, weus ask fuh 'em
In de Nam' uh JE'sus, Amen!

'Enwe nisay 'tankya' Lawd! Yes'suh! T'ank ya 'Lawd! T'ank ya' Lawd!
T'ankya'!

Gwine 'Ta De Mastah!

Our Forefathers Prayed

*"I will lift up mine eyes unto the hills, from whence cometh my help.
My help cometh from the LORD, which made heaven and earth."*
Psalm 121:1-2

*"Be anxious for nothing; but in everything by prayer and supplication
with thanksgiving let your requests be made known unto God."*
Philippians 4:6

*"I will lift up mine eyes unto the hills, from whence cometh my help.
My help cometh from the LORD, which made heaven and earth."*
Psalm 121:1-2

I's gwine ta de Mastah!
Gwine tah mah Lawd
Jesus! Dat's wha' I's gwine
do.

Umm hum! I's gwine ta de Mastah!
Cuz I kin't do it by mesef, no hi
Mi's well gibitta Him
He de Almighty One! He de One wit da plan,
And He sho'nuf got de pow'r!

Yessuh! De good Lawd? He kin han'lit!
Bettah den ainybidy ebbah, ebbah could,
enehi! Tank'ya! Tank'ya! Tank 'ya Jesus!

Chillen,

WALKIN' WID' DAH LAWD

"In all thy ways acknowledge him, and he shall direct thy paths."
Proverbs 3:6

'Effen dah LAWD say move, denyah move!
But 'effen He ain't sayin' nuttin,
Den' bruthah, yah jes stand ri' deh! 'En pray!
Don'cha Gee, nah Haw, lessen dah LAWD say so.

'En when de Good LAWD say suppin'
Den mo'en ye ah know…
Not jes ye by ye'sef,
He'ah gi' yah witness, sho 'nuf.
And ebbah thing 'ah line up wid His Word.

'Caus 'yah always wan'dah LAWD 'tah smile on 'yah!
An' 'yah needhem 'tah be wid'yah, ebbah wa' 'yah go,
Wed'dah 'tis ri' heah… or ovuh de'auh…
An' 'yah wanhem 'tah alwa'tah bless 'yah ebbah time,
Ni'. Dats all…. I gwine say 'bout dat! Umm-humm!

Testafyin'

"In every thing give thanks: for this is the will of God in Christ Jesus concerning you."

1 Thessalonians 5:18

Giv'n honor tah God, whose de Head uh me life;
To mah Lawd, 'en Sav'yah Jesus Christ,
De author, an' de finisher uh mi faith!
"An tah all dos tah who honor due!

I wanna 'tank mah good Lawd fuh hi He wak'n me up dis monin'
Clos in mi a-rit' mind,
Dat mah kivers wa'nt mah wind'n shield
'An mah bed wa'nt mah coolin' boad!
I sho nuf t'ank 'Im! Hi He tech 'en heal mah body
Frum day tah day! T'ank 'ya Jesus!

'An uh t'ank mah good Lawd fan bein' save, en sanctify,
Um on mah way tah glory,
'An ain't nuttin' gon' tu'n me roun'!
Cuz uh mean He'bn ebbah step uh de way!

I wan' ebbah bi'dy who kno' de wuth uh prayer
Dos ur 'ya who kno hi tah git a pray thru'
Tah pray fah me, en mah fam'ly
Dat de good Lawd bless me on mah jurney,
Cuz uh do mean tah mak He'bn mah Home!
T'ank 'ya Jesus! T'ank 'ya good Mas-tah, T'ank 'ya!

Testafyin'

'En Uthah Wourds...

Giving honor to God, who is the Head of my life;
To my Lord and Saviour, Jesus Christ,
The author, and the finisher of my Faith!
Giving honor to my PAS-tor; and all whom honor is due!

I want to thank my good Lord for how He woke me up this morning,
Closed in my right mind.
That my covers weren't my winding shield,
And my bed was not my cooling board!
I sure enough thank Him for how He touch and heal my body
From day to day! Thank you Jesus!

And I thank my good Lord for being saved, and sanctified,
I'm on my way to glory.
And nothing's going to turn me around!
Because I mean Heaven every step of the way!

I want everybody who knows the worth of prayer,
Those of you who know how to get a prayer through;
To pray for me, and my family, that the good Lord
Bless me on my journey; because I do mean to make
Heaven my home! Thank You Jesus!
Thank you good Master, Thank You!

Ain't Gon' Fite Wid' Yah

"And be ye kind one to another, tenderhearted, forgiving one another, even as God for Christ's sake hath forgiven you."

Ephesians 4:32

You be mah brothuh,
En you be mah sistah;
So ain't gon' fite wid yah,
NawSuh!
Ain't gon' fite wid mah fam'ly!

Gon' take care ya,
Hepya all I kin;
Pray fuh ya, smile wid ya,
Ebbah ni' en den, gi' ya a great big grin!

Ya know, de good Lawd?
He bless me wid ya,
Me, needuh you, had nuttin' te do wid dat!
So wha' we gon' fite fuh …
Beatin' air, jes' ta hurt one nuddah?
Cuz at de en' uh de day,
We still be sistahs, an' brothuhs!
We still be fam'ly.

Sho', we k'ant always see eye de eye 'bout ebbah ting!
Cuz God don' bless us wid de good mind tah "t'ink fuh yo' SEF"
Sotah fite? Naw Suh!
Wha' we gon' do dat fuh?
Jes' les hep one nuddah,
Tah go bit fuddah on dis heah life jurney,
Doin' fuh one nuddah wha's good, 'en wha's rite.

Ni' de wurl wud nebber, nebber understan'
Hi' sistahs en brothuhs kin git lawng lak dat;
But dat's fuh dem ta figguh out,
En fuh we tah jes keep on mi'chin' up de King's hi-way,
Encourgin' one nuddah, en doin' fuh one nuddah,
En sho'n tah de whol' wide wurl,
We be Sistahs, En we be Brothuhs ...
En dat's dat!
Amen. Tank ya Jesus!

Chillun, Yennun Blessed!

What My Gran-Me' Would Say

"For the vision is yet for an appointed time, but at the end it whall speak, and not lie: Though it tarry, wait for it; because it will surely come, it will not tarry."

Habbakuk2:3

God don' bless ya'll chillun
To cum'a long way!
From pullin' taters from de tater patch,
En hoe'n cotton,
En shukin' cone,
En bakin' Miss Ann bread …
Yessuh! God don' bless all mah chillun!

Yennun don' gwine on tah school,
And ya' got all dat good larnin' cause ya' studied hard;
Always wan' it tah see yennun make it,
An' um mighty proud uh ya', Yessuh! Mighty proud!
An' for all dat, I sho' nuf praise mah good Lawd!

Well, yennun, wha' ya' gon' do wit ya' blessin' ni?
Thro' it all way? Oh no chillun, don' thro' dem good blessins way!
Tak' de Lawd's blessins 'en do suppin' wit 'em, heah?
Yessuh! God don' bless all mah chillun!

Yea, thou shalt see thy children's children,
and peace upon Israel.
Psalm 128:8.

God Speaks To My Heart

Date:

Scripture Text:

Scripture Text:

My Reflections / Prayer Request:

Life ...
And Living

Hast thou not known?
Hast thou not heard,
That the everlasting God, the Lord,
The creator of the ends of the earth,
Fainteth not, neither is weary?

There is no searching of his
understanding.
He giveth power to the faint;
And to them that hath no might
He increaseth strength.

Even the youths shall faint and be weary,
and the young men shall utterly fall;

But they that wait upon the Lord shall renew
their strength;
They shall mount up with wings as eagles;
They shall run, and not be weary;
And they shall walk, and not faint.'
Isaiah 40:28-31

Teenagers!

"Both young men, and maidens, old men and children: Let them praise the Name of the Lord, for his Name alone is excellent; His glory above the earth and heaven."

Psalm 148:12-13

Teenagers!
Yup! We are, let's say … maturing!
Got our own say-so about everything,
Even our friends think like us, we do have opinions.

Teenagers!
Our Momma, the very creative seamstress she is,
Listens as we describe to her this certain outfit
We've just got to have!
Then she'd lay out and cut the pattern, for a custom fit.

Teenagers!
That skirt and blouse has got to match
And they must fit exactly right;
Handbag, shoes, and of course the scarf
The chain necklace, penny loafers, and bobby socks.

Teenagers!
Very soon our Momma sees what's needed;
So, she hands us the sewing machine, thread and needle;
And with her guidance we girls are now on our way,
Coordinating our own outfits, and looking good, every day!

Teenagers!
At thirteen, we wear our stockings and "high heels" to church;
Good looking dresses and two piece suits..
Not just a skirt and blouse on Sunday ... oh no, never!
Gloves, a pretty purse, matching pumps,
Sometimes a hat, looking really cute!

Teenagers!
We "eye" the boys (a little)
Giggling, and then a whisper, "Oh he likes me!"
Little notes get passed in church ... while the singing's going on:
"I love you, do you love me?", he would write.
"Check yes or no, or maybe, either one."

Teenagers!
Sometimes there's even a note from a friend ...
"Do you see how Sister Quarterdimes fling her arms when shoutin'?
Just picture a squawking, flying chicken, or a duck when it's poutin'."
Response: "Girl, you know ducks don't fly!"
Oh mercy! Can't laugh in church ... oh me, oh my!
Got to be sophisticated..
It's killing our sides, trying to hold that chuckle,
Oh help us, Lord! The laughter's gon' make us buckle!

Teenagers!
Oops! The preacher gets a hold to us!
"You got to be saved," we hear him say,
"No foolishness in church, this is God's house!
Got to be respectful, obey the older folks;
After all, you might be teenagers,
But you're sure not grown!"

Teenagers!
We girls would all get together, and go for afternoon walks
Down the lane, talking and laughing about any and everything;
Sharing ideas, discussing issues, talking about boys, even the Lord!
Then we'd go to 6:00 youth meeting,
And lastly, the Sunday evening service.

Being a teenager?
All a part of "growing up"
And it was o.k. fun!

Youth Progress For Christ

"Train up a child in the way he should go; and when he is old, he will not depart from it."

Proverbs 22:6

The Meeting

We're having a meeting!
Calling it a young people's "Rap Session"
Put together by our Daddy,
Now a minister, over the church Youth;
He invites pastors and ministers of other churches, too.

So, all of us "young people",
Members of congregations throughout the city, Come
together this one Saturday night, With our parents, our
pastors, deacons and preachers To express ourselves:
what we think, what we believe.

Validated, and Valued

And would you know! Those grownups actually
listened! They hear every word, showing genuine concern
In understanding our viewpoint, not "pointing fingers".

This made us teenagers, us "young people"
Feel so important, and all included, As we
were empowered to organize, Electing our
officers, our own age and size.

We make the decision, with our mentors' help
To meet once a month, every fourth Saturday
To express ourselves as elected officials,
To sing, to display our talents,
To develop our leadership and organizational skills.

Getting Together

We rotate every fourth Saturday
From church to church, throughout the city
Having our Business Meetings
With our own officers, making "great" decisions.

Then we sing in groups, and solos and duets,
Also recitations, which were always the"best"
And we all combine to make one big choir,
Becoming known as "Youth Progress For Christ".

Connected, Bonded, and Grounded

Such excitement! and great anticipation,
As the fourth Saturday approached
For us teenagers to get together
In our own meeting, with our parents' support;
To sing, to talk, to discuss God's word;
To hear preaching with us in mind,
Our growth to promote.

Getting black and white uniforms, and taking trips;
Remembering to be "Christ Centered" with any idea;
We young people became forever bonded,
Even years later, still connected, still grounded.

It was the Youth Progress For Christ
That proved the "Shining Light"
That guided us, and steadied our life;
That empowered us to be God fearing teenagers,
To give our best, even our life, to Jesus, Our God, our Creator.

God Speaks To My Heart

Date:

Scripture Text:

Scripture Text:

My Reflections/Prayer Request:

Classmates!

"I thank my God upon every remembrance of you"

Philippians 1:3

Classmates!
From first grade through the twelth:
Reading and Writing, Language and History;
Math and Science, and Music Appreciation;
Algebra and Geometry, Fine Arts, Latin and Physics!

Our teachers were great role models
As they walked before us;
Would let us get by with absolutely nothing!
They groomed us girls to become refined young ladies,
And the boys to become decent, responsible young men;
For our teachers somehow saw "greatness" in our future,
Or was it their "reports" we feared, To our Daddys and our Mommas?

We classmates? Very involved in "extra curricular" activities,
From the school chorus, to the concert and marching bands,
From the Student Council,
To the school newspaper and yearbook staff;
From Girl Scouts and Brownies, to the 4-H Club,
And Future Business Leaders of America;
To cheerleaders … and sports, piano and voice.
We were separated at times by these varied activities,
But still we always had a way to be connected!

Classmates!
Once graduated, and destined to go our separate ways,
Off to college, trade school, armed forces, And eventually marriage;
But after many years, if we should meet, on any given day,
We discovered our "classmate connection" had not gone away!

Such warm, glowing feelings of delight!
When we old friends would meet again,
Whether day or night;
Even after many years, and obvious maturity,
We still remain connected, still classmates, truly!

Graduation Day!

"Now unto him who is able to do exceeding abundantly above all we can ask or think, according to the power that worketh in us."

Ephesians 3:20

It's Graduation Day!
Twelth grade! And we made it!!!!
Got on my cap and gown,
Nervous, yes …
But I'm here! Standing in line.

The processional begins,
We straighten up, ready to march in,
This moment, this day
For which we worked so hard
Is finally here, made it to the End!

All the studying, and going to class,
All the testing, to be sure we pass;
But even through all that,
We classmates still had a blast!

It was worth it, now we can see,
Just to be able to stand in this line
As high school graduates,
Yes!! We now shall be!

We sing our Alma Mater,
"Dear Johnson High" …
Suddenly, tears spring into our eyes;
Our hearts race with rapid beats!
Feeling this love for our school,
With memories running deep.

Our classmate, the Valedictorian,
Gives her grand, resounding speech;
Then we all stand, each name to be called,
"Please let me hear my name, Oh please, dear Lord!"

Hallelujah!
My name is called!
So, I march across the stage,
Walking absolutely straight, and very tall.

Momma and Daddy, family and friends.
My Gran-Me' too,
All present, and cheering
As I graduate from high school!

It's Graduation Day!
Achievements, accolades, lovely gifts;
So many smiles, and sighs of relief,
Happy that we classmates didn't go adrift.

Joyful handclaps to celebrate!
Sending us forth to life's next phase:
College, the military, the workplace,
And then of course, marriage…
Our Wedding Day!

High school graduates …
Taking our place in this Great Big World,
Taking our place,
To make a difference.

Rejoice! Soar!

"But they that wait upon the LORD shall renew their strength; they shall mount up with wings as eagles; they shall run, and not be weary, and they shall walk, and not faint."

Isaiah 40:31

"Rejoice in the Lord always: and again I say, Rejoice." Philippians 4:4

Rejoice! Soar!
On mountains high; The Lord is with you!
Celebrating your victories;
Laughing heartily with you,
Clapping hands with you;,
Leaping from height to height,
Basking in Heaven's liberties.

Rejoice! Soar!
In valleys deep;
The Lord is with you!
Soothing you, walking with you,
Holding your hand,
Providing assurance,
Covering with His Divine Presence
To see you through.

Rejoice! Soar!
Through life's challenges,
The Lord is with you!

So listen closely …
Allow God to lead;
Then your choices will be right,
Your decisions will be just
As in His Holy Word you put your trust.

God Speaks To My Heart

Date:

Scripture Text:

Scripture Text:

My Reflections / Prayer Request:

Getting Real With God ...

"For we have not an high priest which cannot be touched with the feeling of our infirmities, but was in all points tempted like as we are, yet without sin.

Let us therefore come boldly unto the throne of grace, that we may obtain mercy, and find grace to help in time of need."
Hebrews 4:15-16

The Lord, My Strength

"The Lord is my strength, and he will make my feet like hinds feet, and he will make me to walk upon my high places." Habakkuk 3:19

The Lord is my strength!
His Precious Blood for me powerful to heal
Every pain, every wound, every broken place;
As before Him, my God I kneel,
Receiving His love, receiving His grace.

The Lord is my strength!
Making me sure-footed in slippery places;
And in my life He shows himself great
As I move and operate within His grace.

The Lord is my strength!
Bringing down every obstacle, every high place
Clearing the way, opening the gates,
Placing me within His Divine Order
As powerful ways, for me, He makes.

The Lord is my strength!
And in His Name I shall go forth,
Extending dreams and visions to the greatest length
From east to west, from south to north.

My Classmate, My Friend

Today, I saw my classmate, my friend
Who greeted me with a great big smile;
A smile that said, "Hello! Glad to see you;
It's been a long time, a really long while."

My classmate, my friend
We both laughed,
Remembering the good times we shared
As we talked … yes, it was honest talk;
Didn't matter,
We just talked through the happy,
Through the sad.

We looked each other in the eye,
Expressions of sincerity, that said it all;
No issues to "walk around", nothing to hide,
As we remembered the good 'ole days,
When we both stood so tall!

My classmate, my friend,
Still tall and handsome, sure of himself;
I reflect, remembering it was somewhat a "trend"
As he "wooed[7]" the ladies, including myself!

But my God had a greater plan!
For me, oh yes, for my life;
And it was God Himself who took my hand,
Guiding me into His will, into His Purpose,
My Everlasting Life.

And so now, my Classmate, My friend,
I release you, again!
To SOAR HIGH In wonderful freedom!
To experience more of God, your Divine Creator;
To be all you were meant to become
As I pray for you … and at times recall
The sweet moments, the hearty laughter,
The lovely memories.

Can God Trust You?

"Trust in the Lord with all thine heart, and lean not to thine own understanding; In all thy ways acknowledge Him, and He shall direct thy paths."

Proverbs 3:5-6

You say you love the Lord,
With all your heart;
But will you walk with Him
And from His Will, never deviate, nor depart?

Can the Lord trust you,
To say the right words
To that one who "took you through"
To have the courage to heal their hurt
As you rest in God, to Him remaining true?

Can the Lord trust you
To go, and love that soul with God's love,
Showing compassion …
Realizing your own human frailty
Comes through victory only from heaven, above?

Can the Lord trust you
To hold that hand in purity, in honest sincerity,
Void of any devious motives, but only truth;
To support them, and pray for them,
Determined to see them through?

You say you love the Lord …
Really?!!!
Then take to yourself some courage!
Show the Lord, walk with God
As you take your heavenly Father's hand,
That giant step of faith,
Leaning upon His Holy Word!

You say you love the Lord …
Really?!! Really …
Then Go … tell that one about Jesus,
How He had mercy on you,
Saved you from your sin;
That they, too, can be set free through Christ,
And Eternal Life, to win!

At The Altar

OH LORD, BLESS ME!

"And he said, I will not let thee go, except thou bless me." Genesis 32:26

Lord, here's me! I'm here,
Laying on this altar
With my life, my desires, my goals,
Here's my all, Lord here's me.

Lord, you've always been with me, all my life,
During all my joys, all my pain, even during the "fight";
You've been my refuge, my strength,
Standing by my side, being my defense.

You've brought me to success,
And through so many tests!
You saw me through every season,
Knowing for me what's always best.

But this right here, Lord? It's a BIG one!
And to do it your way, I honestly do not want.
The pain's hit my heart, and it hurts so bad;
The struggle to surrender my feelings …
Well, it's making me truly sad.

So, I'm kneeling right here,
Down at the cross, here at this altar;
And I'm releasing it all to you;
Taking a while, but I'm letting go,
Can't go down the road of mistakes no more.

Lord, I can't do a thing without you!
You must go with me,
And in front of me, too;
Won't make not one move unless you agree;
So here's me, at this altar Lord,
Down at Calvary... here at your feet.

Yes, Lord, I'm staying right here,
Until you bless me;
Until I know for sure I'm truly free;
This pain, this ache, this hurt, even my own pride,
I'm laying it all down before you,
With nothing to hide.

So, here's me, Lord
Laying here, on this altar...
Here's my all... Oh My heavenly Father!
Bless me, help me, take away every falter!

And then Lord!
I'll surely praise you,
And give your name the glory!
For cleansing me through and through,
With your precious blood, shed for me at Calvary,
Your precious blood, setting me really truly free!

God Speaks To My Heart

Date:

Scripture Text:

Scripture Text:

My Reflections/Prayer Request:

Sista Friend

LET IT GO!

*"But **grow in grace, and in the knowledge of our Lord and Saviour Jesus Christ To him be glory both now and forever. Amen." 2 Peter 3:18***

Sista Friend,
I know you're hurt, and really angry, my Sista,
Anger that reaches back for decades, many years;
For somehow there was never for you an avenue
For you to talk, to vent your fears.

So, Sista Friend,
You just carried it within yourself
The best way you knew how;
Wasn't always God's way - you know that!
You just did it your way, you buried your sorrow.

Sista Friend,
In carrying your own weight, your own burden
This crippled and maimed your spirit, raising up your "iron curtain"
And when you finally, finally came out
It was with loudness, and rudeness, and cruelty;
It was with devious acts, a mischievous hand,
All efforts of defense, to "be in control" You were trying to bring.

Oh my Sista Friend!
There were times you had to "paste" on a smile
Your hugs and your handshake a tell-tale sign
That surely there was some bitterness lying deep inside,
Veiled through the "growl" of your voice, the "smirk" in your smile.

Yes, Sista Friend,
At times, you even tried the "Big Bully" game
Appearing to be 'Tough", and Respect to "gain"
But this only increased your own pain,
As that ploy, too, failed to help you win.

Sista Friend,
Here's the secret for your healing, for really true success!
Forgiveness brings sweetness,
Which flows from God's heart of love
As unforgiveness, and bitterness (for whatever reason)
Is released, and relinquished, to our God above!

So Sista friend,
Let it go! Just let it go...
Give it all to God, onto Him your cares throw;
He'll gladly take your burdens, all your issues
Then cover with His blood, giving you the victory!

Come on, Sista Friend!
Let it go! Just let it go ...
Jesus already carried your sorrow,
Took all your pain, and every woe;
He did that way back on Calvary,
Before you even knew your name!

And so my Sista Friend,
Go on! Give it all to Him,
The One who made the way
For your peace, your joy, your happiness,
Release it now, in Jesus' Name!

RELEASE
Let all bitterness, and wrath, and anger, and clamour,
and evil speaking, be put away from you, with all malice;

And be ye kind one to another, tenderhearted, forgiving
one another, even as God for Christ's sake hath forgiven you.
Ephesians 4:31-32

Sweet Surrender: Break-Through!

"And the very God of peace sanctify you wholly; and I pray God your whole spirit and soul and body be preserved blameless unto the coming of our Lord Jesus Christ. Faithful is he that calleth you, who also will do it."

1 Thessalonians 5:23-24

So easy, so relaxed,
So free, no "acts"
All because I came to you, My Lord,
Asking for your help, I went to the "max".

You poured your healing oil upon me,
Allowing your Holy Spirit to flow freely
Through every area of my being,
Filling with your love, your forgiveness.

Oh! My Lord, and my God!
Would it that everybody knew you as LORD!
That you are truly our salvation, our deliverer,
Able to handle every weight, free every sin,
Lift every burden.

Come, my dear sister! Come my dear brother!
Come to the altar of the Most High God;
Give Him your cares, your issues,
Give Him your life, your all;
He will gladly take it,
And in exchange give you peace,
And joy, ultimate freedom!

God Speaks To My Heart

Date:

Scripture Text:

Scripture Text:

My Reflections/Prayer Request:

*The Lord will perfect that which
concerneth me:
Thy mercy, O Lord, endureth
forever: forsake not the works of
thine own hands.
Psalm 138:8*

*But the God of all grace,
Who hath called us unto his eternal
glory by Christ Jesus,
after that ye have suffered a while,
make you perfect,
stablish, strengthen, settle you.
1 Peter 5:10*

Father, Forgive Them!

Bullying & Mistreatment

"Then said Jesus, Father, forgive them, for they know not what they do".
Luke 23:34

Our Lord Jesus was crucified upon a cruel cross,
He hung there, as a convicted criminal;
But He was innocent!

And He said,
"Father, forgive them, for they know not what they do;
They were moving Him into Triumphant Victory!

He was accused of blasphemy, treated as a "rebel"
They spit in his face, slapped and shoved him;
But He had done no wrong!

And he said,
"Father, forgive them, for they know not what they do;
They were moving him into Triumphant Victory!

They "mocked" Him, throwing a purple robe around Him,
Crushed a thorny "crown" of briers upon his brow,
Producing intense pain, gushing forth profuse bleeding;
They accused Him of high treason "Blasphemy!"
Lashing out hurt to His spirit; pain to His heart;

And yet He prayed,
"Father forgive them, for they know not what they do;
They were moving Him into Triumphant Victory!

They jabbed a razor-sharp spear into his side
While steadying his hands and his feet,
Banging in to them, huge iron nails,
Spilling his precious pure Blood …
For you, for me.

Oh, the precious Blood of Jesus! that bought for us redemption,
Paying the price with his own life, To set us guilty sinners free!

As he prayed,
"Father forgive them,
They know not what they do";
They were moving Purpose,
Bringing forth Destiny,
Moving our Lord into Triumphant Victory!

Triumphant Victory!

Over Abuse And/Or Rejection

"He is despised and rejected of men; a man of sorrows, and acquainted with grief: and we hid as it were our faces from him; he was despised, and we esteemed him not. Surely he hath born our griefs, and carried our sorrows: yet we did esteem him stricken, smitten of God, and afflicted."
Isaiah 53:3-4

They condemned our Lord Jesus,
Hung Him on Calvary's cross;
How could they have been capable
Of such vicious cruelty?

They, because of their unbelief,
Ventured into …
Misunderstanding, which led to confusion
Confusion, which led to bitterness,
Bitterness, which led to jealousy
Jealousy, which led to anger,
Anger, which led to hatred,
Hatred, which led to malice
Malice, which led to vindictiveness
And bitter vindictiveness,
Which drove them to ugly plots and schemes…

And obstructing justice,
Using their concocted "legal"
system, They passed the
sentence: "Death by Crucifixion"

But our Lord Jesus was innocent!
He had done no wrong.
Yet he prayed, "Father forgive them,
For they know not what they do."
They were moving Him into Triumphant Victory!

And so now, for those who have inflicted injury,
Let us pray for God to touch their hearts,
And bring them to repentance,
As we allow our own hearts to pray:

Heavenly Father, in the Name of Jesus,
Forgive them, for they don't understand..
And forgive me, too, for causing any harm or pain,
As I'm being moved toward my destiny,
According to God's Divine Plan;:
To be a walking example of God's grace and power in the earth,
Winning multitudes of lost souls into the Kingdom of God;
Moving with God into Triumphant Victory!

Trust God!

Psalm 37:1-11
**Fret not thyself because of evildoers, neither be thou
envious against the workers of iniquity.**

For they shall soon be cut down like the grass, and wither as the green herb.

**Trust in the LORD, and do good: so shalt thou dwell
in the land, and verily thou shalt be fed.**

Delight thyself also in the LORD, and he shall give the desires of thine heart.

**Commit thy way unto the LORD; trust also
in him; and he shall bring it to pass.**

*And he shall bring forth thy righteousness as the
light, and thy judgment as the noonday,*

**Cease from anger, and forsake wrath; fret
not thyself in any wise to do evil.**

*For evildoers shall be cut off; but those that wait upon
the LORD, they shall inherit the earth.*

Rest in the LORD, and wait patiently for him; fret not thyself...
*For yet a little while, and the wicked shall not be; yea
thou shalt diligently consider his place, and it shall not be.*

**But the meek shall inherit the earth; and
shall delight themselves in the
abundance of peace.**

BE HEALED!

*Be anxious for nothing; but in everything by prayer and supplication
with thanksgiving let your requests be made known unto God.*

*And the peace of God, which passeth all understanding, shall
keep your hearts and minds through Christ Jesus.*

*Finally brethren, Whatsoever things are true; whatsoever things
are honest; whatsoever things are just; whatsoever things are pure;
whatsoever things are lovely; whatsoever things are of good report; if
there be any virture, and if there be any praise, think on these things.*
Philippians 4:6-8

God Speaks To My Heart

Date:

Scripture Text:

Scripture Text:

My Reflections /Prayer Request:

The Lord that made heaven and earth bless thee out of Zion.
Psalm 134:3

HEALING : RENEWAL

And be renewed in the spirit of your mind;
And that ye put on the new man, which after God is
created in righteousness and true holiness.

Wherefore putting away lying, speak every man truth
to his neighbor; for we are members one of another;

Be ye angry, and sin not: let not the sun go down upon
your wrath; Neither give place to the devil.

Let him that stole steal no more; but rather let
him labour, working with his hands the thing which is
good, that he may have to give to him that needeth.

Let no corrupt communication proceed out of your
mouth, but tht which is good to the use of edifying, that
it may minister grace unto the hearers.

And grieve not the holy Spirit of God,
whereby ye are sealed unto the day of redemption.
Ephesians 4:23-30

God's Assurance: "I Am With You!"

"and lo, I am with you always, even unto the end of the world. Amen."
St. Matthew 28:20b

ENJOY LIFE… LIVE! SING A SONG! WALK IN FORGIVENESS…
"For His merciful kindness is great toward us" Psalm 117:2
"And forgive us our debts, as we forgive our debtors" Matthew 6:12

TAKE COURAGE! WALK TALL! GOD IS YOUR STRENGTH!
"I will go in the strength of the Lord God" Psalm 71:16
"Be of good courage, and he shall strengthen your heart" Psalm 31:24
"The Lord is my strength and my song, and is become my salvation" Psalm 118:14

GROW A GARDEN! SEE GOD'S BEAUTY… EXPERIENCE GROWTH!
"Let all the people praise thee O God… then shall the earth yield her increase, and God, even our own God, shall bless us" Psalm 67:5-6
"But grow in grace, and in the knowledge of our Lord and Saviour Jesus Christ" 2 Peter 3:18

"God is our refuge and strength, a very present help..." Psalm 46:1

LIGHTEN YOUR HEART! SMILE! LAUGH HEARTILY!
"A merry heart doeth good like a medicine" Proverbs 17:22a
"Casting all your care upon Him, for He careth for you" 1 Peter 5:7

READ WHOLESOME BOOKS! WATCH WHAT YOU SAY!
"Thy word is a lamp unto my feet, and a light unto my path."

Psalm 119:105

"Pleasant words are as an honeycomb, sweet to the soul, and health to the bones."

Proverbs 16:24

BE COMPASSIONATE... LOVE! GIVE... AND SHARE!
"How good and how pleasant it is for brethren to dwell together in unity."
Psalm 133:1

"And be ye kind one to another, tenderhearted, forgiving one
another, even as God for Christ's sake hath forgiven you."

Ephesians 4:32

"For I was an hungred, and ye gave me meat: I was thirsty, and
ye gave me drink: I was a stranger, and ye took me in: Naked,
and ye clothed me: I was sick, and ye visited me: I was in prison,
and ye came unto me."

St. Matthew 25:35-36

God Speaks To My Heart

"I will never leave thee, nor forsake thee."

Hebrews 13:5b

As life's challenges take you over mountains high,
Even through valleys, wide and deep,
I will be with you, every day, every hour,
Providing you my strength, my power.

As the task I've assigned you makes you weary,
My Spirit, my Comforter, I've given you,
My assurance and promise, that I'm with you
And your burdens I do gladly carry.

I provide my pillow, the Word of God,
On which to lay your head;
As my holy angels surround you
With melodies sweet, to soothe you,
To relieve you of any dread.

My child, it is my Word that has carried you!
For the words I speak, are Spirit and Life;
And it is my Word that will abide with you
From earth, through the grave,
Quickening you into Eternal Life!

"Looking unto Jesus the author and finisher of our faith; who for the joy that was set before him endured the cross, despising the shame, and is set down at the right hand of the throne of God."
Hebrews 12:2

Love ...
God's Greatest
Gift!

Love: The More Excellent Way

1 Corinthians 13:1-13

Though I speak with the tongues of men and of angels,
And have not charity,
I am become as sounding brass,
Or a tinkling cymbal.

And though I have the gift of prophecy And understand all mysteries,
And all knowledge;
And though I have all faith,
So that I could remove mountains,
And have not charity,
I am nothing.

And though I bestow all my goods to feed the poor, And though I give my body to be burned, And have not charity, It profiteth me nothing.

Charity suffereth long, And is kind; Charity envieth not; Charity vaunteth not itself, Is not puffed up.

Doth not behave itself unseemly, Seeketh not her own, Is not easily provoked, Thinketh no evil; Rejoiceth not in iniquity, But rejoiceith in the truth;

Beareth all things, Believeth all things, Hopeth all things, Endureth all things;

Now abideth faith, hope, charity, these three; But the greatest of these is charity.

Lord, Give Me Your Heart!

"And Jesus went forth, and saw a great multitude, and was moved with compassion toward them, and healed their sick." Matthew 14:14

To touch,
To love,
To bring a smile,
To relieve a hurt;
Oh Lord, give me your heart!

To bring joy,
To produce happiness,
To bring calm,
To insure peace;
Oh Lord, give me your heart!

To love laughter,
To relieve stress,
To bless with kind words,
To encourage with a hug;
Oh Lord, give me your heart!

To wipe away a tear,
To calm the frazzled nerves,
Allowing one to laugh,
Yes, to chuckle again..
Oh Lord, give me your heart!

To open my ears to another's cry,
To open my heart to another's care,
To open my hands to relieve despair,
Oh Lord, give me your heart!

For God so loved the world, that He gave
His only begotten Son, that whosoever
believeth in Him should not perish, but have
everlasting life.
For God sent not His Son into the world to
condemn the world, but that the world
through Him might be saved.
St. John 3:16-17

Hey, Friend! You Saved?

Wherefore he is able to save them to the uttermost that come unto God by him, seeing he ever liveth, to make intercession for them."
Hebrews 6:25

Hey, Friend!
You saved, yet?
Have you given your life to Jesus,
Been set free from your sins?

Hey, My Friend!
Yesterday's gone,
And tomorrow may never come;
Today's here, Now ...
You make the decision, it's your life, any how!

My Friend!
There really is a beautiful Heaven,
Where you can live in peace and joy, forever!
But there's also a fiery hell
Where you can live in misery and torment, forever!

Hey, my Friend!
It's up to you – make now your decision.
We all, yes every one of us, were born sinners.
But through Jesus Christ our Lord and Saviour,
We all can be winners! Our Lord and Saviour
Gave His life for me, and for you,
Just so we can be born again... start our life anew.

You, My Friend,
Was on God's mind, the whole time!
Even when you didn't know it, He loved you,
And for you, He gave His only Son to die;
But our Lord Jesus got up from the grave …
He actually rose up from the dead!
And He's alive, right now, this very moment,
With victory in His hand!

Hey, My Friend!
Come to Jesus, Now!
Nothing, or no one, is worth going
To an eternal, fiery hell for, no how!
Be your own man, be your own woman
Make the right decision, Come to Jesus!
And be free, evermore!

"The LORD ... is longsuffering to usward, not willing that any should perish, but that all should come to repentance,." 2 Peter 3:9

Romans 10:9
That if thou shalt confess with thy mouth the Lord
Jesus, and shall believe in thine heart that God hath
raised him from the dead, thou shalt be saved.

Acts 2:36b-39
God hath made that same Jesus, whom ye have
crucified, both Lord and Christ,

Now when they heard this, they were pricked in
their heart, and said unto Peter and to the rest of the
apostles, men and brethren, what shall we do?

Then Peter said unto them, repent, and be
baptized everyone of you in the name of Jesus Christ
for the remission of sins, and ye shall receive
the gift of the Holy Ghost.

For the promise is unto you, and to your children,
and to all that are afar off, even as many as the Lord
our God shall call.

God Speaks To My Heart

Date:

My Reflections / Prayer Request:

Scripture Text

Scripture Text

*"Whoso findeth a wife findeth a good thing, and
obtaineth favour of the Lord."*
Proverbs 18:22

***

"The voice of my beloved!
Behold, he cometh leaping upon the mountains,
skipping upon the hills.

My beloved is like a roe or a young hart:
behold, he standeth behind our wall,
he looketh forth at the windows,
shewing himself through the lattice.

My beloved spake, and said unto me,
Rise up, my love, my fair one, and come away.

For lo, the winter is past, the rain is over and gone;
The flowers appear on the earth;
the time of the singing of birds is come,
and the voice of the turtle is heard in our land;

The fig tree putteth forth her green figs,
and the vines with the tender grape give a good smell.

Arise my love, my fair one, and come away."
Song Of Solomon 2:1-4, 8-13

Engaged!

"Delight thyself also in the LORD: and he shall give thee the desires of thine heart."

Psalm 37:4

I'm engaged!!! Getting married!
See my Diamond!
Proudly extending my hand for all to see:
Family, friends, anybody!
Such a wonderful, special, glowing feeling
Being in love, and chosen,
And now, a bride-to-be!

Been praying and waiting for the day
When I'd walk down the aisle
On my wedding day;
A beautiful bride — happy, oh so happy!
God really answered my prayer,
My desire he gave.

I'm engaged!!! Getting married!
Found my love, whose name I'll gladly carry;
And to be loved and yes, to be in love,
With the man of my dreams …
Truly a blessing, my gift from God.

Now! To choose that perfect, beautiful wedding dress!
And just the right veil, and those special shoes;
Then to select that elegant "fine" china pattern,
The sparkling crystal stemware, and exquisite silver pieces,
All these, every bride's just got to have, as her joy increases!

I'm engaged!!! Getting married!
Selecting my bridesmaids,
They, too, are happy for me, and full of smiles
As we choose their gowns, and shoes and flowers.

The bridal showers, brand new cookware
And soft, flowing, luxurious lingerie;
Also luncheons and teas, all "social standards"
All to honor me, the glowing and gracious Bride-to-Be!

I'm engaged!! Getting married!
Oh, this glow of sunshine from my very inside,
Reflects all over, especially when I smile!
It's so wonderful to fall in love
Then to marry the one who holds my heart, My true love!

As my Wedding Day approaches,
We all … everybody… are so very happy,
Full of excitement! And anticipation…
Yes! Everybody's filled with glee!

*"…Entreat me not to leave thee, or
to return from following after thee: for
whither thou goest, I will go; and
where thou lodgest, I will lodge: thy
people shall be my people, and thy
God my God"
Ruth 1:16*

Today, I Marry My Love

Wedding Day

"My beloved is mine, and I am his ... " Song of Solomon 2:16a

Today, I will be given in marriage,
To my groom, my husband-to-be;
This man that I love with all my heart!
Such a warm, wonderful sweet feeling
Just floods my very heart, my whole being
With waves and waves of endless love!

Today, I'm getting married!
I'm a Bride! This is my answered prayer;
God through His Word has to me, proven faithful,
And to the Lord, I'm so truly grateful.

Getting the final touch to my new hairdo,
A quick facial, then a manicure and pedicure;
Then to rest in a fragrant, soothing "bubble bath"
To insure I'm all relaxed,
For that glowing look, I just simply must have!

I ease into my Wedding Gown,
So beautiful! So perfect!
Then my bridal veil's gingerly in place,
So elegant, altogether lovely!
Finally, placed into my hands,
A lovely bouquet of fragrant roses!

My maid of honor, even my attendants
Are absolutely radiant ... all smiles!
Their dresses all so colorfully vivid,
With matching hairpieces, and dyed-to-match slippers.

Oh! Today! I marry my Love!
He's so handsome, waiting for me, there at the altar!
He smiles as he sees me. ... A tear bursts into my eyes ...
As I also see him ... and the lighted candles ... the garden scene of flowers.

The music begins. ... it's time!
Lord, please don't let me trip. ... it's a very long aisle!
"Here Comes The Bride!"
The organ and the trumpet begin to play,
Everyone in the church stands
All in honor of me, a lovely Bride!
I feel so beautiful! So full of grace!

My beloved reaches for my hand
And the two of us are now
Together ... at the altar, We're here, in place.

"Dearly Beloved"
The preacher begins,
"We're gathered here today, in the sight of God
To join this man and this woman
In Holy Matrimony".

Oh, oh! Thank you, Jesus!
It's happening, really happening!
My heart's overwhelmed with absolute joy!
I'm being married, his wife I'm becoming!

We exchange our vows, each to the other,
"To have and to hold, from this day forward";
Then to each the other we give a gold ring,
Sealing our promises with a kiss, And our
"love song" we sing.

We kneel together, our hands clasped in prayer,
Believing God, as blessings are asked for us in marriage;
For all our days, to keep us in His care, That in all our
joys, and in sorrow, To be with us there.

"Our Father who art in heaven,
Hallowed be Thy Name,
We thank you for this day,
For our blessed union in marriage."
In the wonderful name of Jesus,
We truly thank you. Amen!

God Speaks To My Heart

Date:

Scripture Text:

Scripture Text:

My Reflections / Prayer Request:

The Heavenly Marriage
Of The Lamb

*And I heard as it were the voice of a great
multitude, and as the voice of many waters, and
as the voice of mighty thunderings, saying,
Alleluia: for the LORD GOD omnipotent
reigneth.*

*Let us be glad and rejoice, and give honour to
him: for the marriage of the Lamb is come, and
his wife hath made herself ready.*

*And to her was granted that she should be
arrayed in fine linen, clean and white: for the
fine linen is the righteousness of saints.*

*And he saith unto me, Write, Blessed are they
which are called unto the marriage supper of
the Lamb. And he saith unto me, These are the
true sayings of GOD.   Revelation 19:6-9*

The Heavenly Bridal March

"Let us be glad and rejoice, and give honour to him: for the marriage of the Lamb is come, and his wife hath made herself ready. And to her was granted that she should be arrayed in fine linen, clean and white: for the fine linen is the righteousness of saints."

Revelation 19:7b -8

Here she comes!
The trumpet rings out the joyous notes
For the grand musical entrance …
The commanding voice of the archangel is heard,
A distinctive, resounding cry;
All heaven stands in full attention,
To receive the long awaited Bride of Christ!

Here she comes!
The Bride of Christ!
Coming through thousands of generations,
The victorious, the triumphant
Church of the Living God!

Here she comes!
The Bride of Christ!
Arrayed in luxurious fine linen
Sparkling pure white as the new-driven snow;
Her beautiful, spotless robe, flowing. … flowing …
Falling softly into lovely voluminous folds,
The triumphant church of the Living God!

Here she comes!
The Bride of Christ!
Her righteousness shines bright as the noon day sun;
Her sparkling golden crown glimmers with bright, radiant stars,
All gleaming reflections of her kingdom work,
With the help of Almighty God, so well done;
The triumphant church of the Living God!

Here she comes!
The Bride of Christ!
Having prepared herself through countless fiery tests and trials,
Refined within the intense fires of life's afflictions
Having walked in victory through the waters, …
Through the floods … through the temptations …
The triumphant church of the Living God!

"Come up hither … come close to me"
Says the Lamb, her Bridegroom, Jesus Christ himself!
"Sit here at my table, here at my right hand …
For this, my marriage supper is sumptuously prepared,
Just for you, my wife, my bride…"
The triumphant church of the Living God!

"Behold! I come quickly! says the Lord,
"And my reward is with me …
To honor you, my bride, my pearl of great price;
Purchased and redeemed with mine own precious blood,
The triumphant, victorious church of the Living God!"

*For this cause shall a man leave
his father and mother, and shall be
joined unto his wife, and they two
shall be one flesh.*

*This is a great mystery: but I speak
concerning Christ and the church.*

*Nevertheless let every one of you
in particular so love his wife, even
as himself; and the wife see that
she reverence her husband.*
Ephesians 5:31-33

Lord, I Love You More!

"I found Him whom my soul loveth"

Song of Solomon 3:4

As I consider how you have blessed my life,
And all I set my heart to do, you have allowed;
But at the end of the day,
Lord, I love you more!

When I realize all that I am
And all that I've ever been,
Is because of your love,
Because of your faithfulness,
Still Lord, I love you more!

As I feel the warmth of your love,
The joy in my soul;
The laughter and smile within my heart,
I know it's because for me you care.
Oh Lord, I love you more!

Thank you Lord, for being my constant friend,
Always there with me in everything;
Even when I make "dumb" decisions,
You step in, granting more of your provisions!

How can I say thanks!
How can I express myself, truly?
I give you my life, to serve only you,
And still oh Lord, I love you more!

"I love the Lord,
because he hath heard my voice
and my supplications.

Because he hath inclined his ear unto me,
therefore will I call upon him
as long as I live."
Psalm 116:1-2

God Speaks To My Heart

Date:

Scripture Text:

Scripture Text:

My Reflections/Prayer Request:

God Speaks To My Heart

Date   **Time**

God Speaks To My Heart

Date   **Time**

"The Lord shall be unto thee an everlasting light,
and thy God thy glory."

"Thou shalt also be a crown of glory in the hand of the Lord,
and a royal diadem in the hand of thy God."
Isaiah 60:20a; 62:3

Brethren,
I count not myself to have
apprehended; but this one
thing I do, forgetting those
things which are behind, and
reaching forth unto those
things which are before.

I press toward the mark for
the prize of the high calling
of God in Christ Jesus.
Philippians 3:13-14

Conclusion

Bernetha Lorick Moultrie

In the beginning, the Almighty God in His infinite wisdom and divine power, created the heaven and the earth. As the Divine Master Craftsman, God, in His illustrious, creative grand style and meticulously organized manner, moved.... by His Spirit. He brought forth the conditions of excellence in the creation; God called forth LIGHT!

"In the beginning God created the heaven and the earth.

And the earth was without form, and void: and darkness was upon the face of the deep. And the Spirit of God moved upon the face of the waters.

And God said, Let there be light; and there was light.

And God saw the light, that it was good; and God divided the light from the darkness.

And God called the light Day, and the darkness he called Night.
And the evening and the morning were the first day.

Genesis 1:1-5

The Spirit of God moved… calling forth the wonder of Order out of utter Chaos; God spoke, and at His word, He divided the waters below (ocean and seas) from the waters above (heavens).

God spoke, and called forth the dry land from out of the deep waters! God spoke, and in the midst of the absolute thick darkness, He called forth LIGHT!

> *"And God said, Let there be lights in the firmament of the heaven to divide the day from the night; and let them be for signs, for seasons, for days, and years.*
>
> *And let them be for lights in the firmament of the heaven to give light upon the earth; and it was so.*
>
> *And God made two great lights; the greater light to rule the day (the sun) and the lesser light to rule the night (the moon); He made the stars also. (billions and billions of stars!)*
>
> *And God set them in the firmament of the heaven to give light upon the earth,*
>
> *And to rule over the day and over the night, and to divide the light from the darkness; and God saw that it was good.*
>
> *And the evening and the morning were the fourth day."*

Genesis 1:14-19

The Almighty God surely knows, and we finite humans must understand, that morning always follows night! It is God Himself who causes light to shine forth out of darkness. Be assured, tomorrow *will* come!

As we follow God's light, trusting Him through this journey called "life"; walking with Him through every season; trusting Him through every trial; believing Him with every test; glorifying Him through every adversity, we through faith in the finished work at Calvary, are to confidently believe, and to follow, the true and living God, Who always has our best interest at heart. The Almighty God in His wisdom and love for mankind, made provision to redeem man from his fallen Adamic state!

> *"For God so loved the world, that He gave His only begotten Son, that whosoever believeth in Him should not perish, but have everlasting life." St. John 3:16*

As we make the choice to believe and take God at His word; and to repent of (turn away from) our sins (transgression against God and against our fellow man); and then receive the Lord Jesus Christ into our life through faith in the finished work of Calvary;   as we choose to walk in the light of God's holy word: His forgiveness, His gentleness, His peace, His tranquility, His goodness, His compassion, His love! We will experience, with the help of the indwelling Holy Spirit, the transforming power of the true and living God in our very life!

> *"For God, who commanded the light to shine out of darkness, hath shined in our hearts, to give the light of the knowledge of the glory of God in the face of Jesus Christ.*
>
> *But we have this treasure in earthen vessels, that the excellence of the power may be of God, and not of us."*
> *2 Corinthians 4:6-7*

Our wonderful Lord can help us see beauty, experience peace, enjoy the simple wonders of living!

And when the night has passed… When Morning Comes… we can see that life truly is good, life is worth living, life is o.k. regardless of the circumstances… because our God is good! Our God knows!

Our God sees! Our God understands! Our God cares!

Be encouraged! Follow the Almighty God… the Light! Follow His true and living Word… the Light!

Receive God's Holy Spirit, the Comforter… the Light! This is our victory, even our faith in our Lord and Saviour, Jesus Christ, and His redemptive work at Calvary. This is the victory for mankind, all the way from earth to glory!

> *"God is light, and in Him is no darkness at all.*
>
> *If we walk in the light, as He is in the light,*
> *We have fellowship with one another, and the*
> *Blood of Jesus Christ His Son cleanseth us from all sin."*
>

1 John 1:5a,7

> *"Looking unto Jesus, the author and finisher of our faith!"*
>

Hebrews 12:2a

Now unto him that is able to
keep you from falling, and to
present you faultless before
the presence of his glory with
exceeding joy,
To the only wise God our
Saviour, be glory and
majesty, dominion and power,
both now and ever. Amen.
Jude 24-25

Acknowledgements

Many thanks, and much appreciation to:

The Almighty God, for His provision and divine help; for His guidance and direction through His Holy Spirit in accomplishing this project.

My beloved late husband, for his unwavering love, and faith in God; for his strong words of encouragement and godly instruction that remain with me still.

My father, "Daddy Bishop", for his apostolic wisdom and godly insight; who recognized God's favor, and who always acknowledged the hand of God upon my life.

Those Bishops and Pastors in ministry who also have been so gracious in embracing my assigned work for the cause of Christ and the kingdom of God.

The Staff at Richland County Public Library for their professional assistance.

The James E. Clyburn Learning Center for the use of their facility.

The Design & Layout Team at AuthorHouse for their professional expertise.

My partners in prayer, for their inspirational support and words of encouragement.

The church ecclesia, the Body of Christ, my "safe haven" for whom I have a special love.

My wonderful family, especially Momma and Daddy, my sisters and brothers, and childhood friends; all who have been a source of warmth and strength all of my life! Thank you.

Author Biography

A native of Columbia, SC Bernetha Moultrie is an Ordained Evangelist with the Pentecostal Assemblies of the World, Inc. She is the Founder and Director of Emmanuel Ministries, Inc. which focuses on intercessory prayer, and promotes and celebrates the successes of our community's youth through their daily application of biblical principles, moral integrity, wholesome Christian living, and academic empowerment. The youth are also encouraged in their character improvement and compassion for others through active community service. She embraces seniors and military veterans who now live in their "golden years" through community outreach and health benefit services. She serves on the ministerial staff in her local church, and serves as Chaplain for the North Columbia Civic Club and the Greenview Reunion Foundation.

Using innovative ways of sharing the salvation gospel of Jesus Christ, she has produced and directed several musical dramas, including "Refined To Shine" and "The Ten Virgins". She is also the author of several writings, including her recently published book of Poetry "Then SINGS! My Heart". She shares God's very relevant word in church services, at conferences, and in community forums. She has produced and hosted the radio show "Word For Today" WLMC Georgetown, SC.

*"One thing have I desired of the Lord,
that will I seek after; that I may dwell
in the house of the Lord all the days
of my life, to behold the beauty of the
Lord, and to enquire in his temple."*
Psalm 27:4